# HANSEL & GRETEL

GRIMM

ILLUSTRATED BY MONIQUE FELIX

CREATIVE EDITIONS

MANKATO

With gratitude and respect I dedicate this special edition of Hansel & Gretel
to the people whose dream made the entire Once Upon A Time collection
a reality. Their unique vision continues to inspire me.

*Tom Peterson*      *15 March 2001*

Illustrations © 1983 Monique Felix

Published in 2001 by Creative Editions

123 South Broad Street, Mankato, MN 56001 USA

Creative Editions is an imprint of The Creative Company

Designed by Rita Marshall

Printed in Italy

Library of Congress Cataloging-in-Publication Data

Hansel und Gretel. English

Hansel and Gretel / written by Jacob and Wilhelm Grimm; illustrated by Monique Felix.

Summary: When they are left in the woods by their parents, two
children find their way home despite an encounter with a wicked witch.

ISBN 1-56846-137-2

[1. Fairy tales. 2. Folklore—Germany.] I. Grimm, Jacob,
1785-1863. II. Grimm, Wilhelm, 1786-1859. III. Felix, Monique, ill. IV. Title.

PZ8. H196 2001      398.2'0943'02—dc21      99-052360

First Edition      5  4  3  2  1

# ONCE UPON A TIME

THERE dwelt at the edge of a large forest a poor woodcutter with his wife and two children; the boy was called Hansel and the girl Gretel. He had little to live on, and once, when there was a great famine in the land, he couldn't even provide them with daily bread. One night, as he was tossing about in bed, full of worry, he sighed and said to his wife:

"What's to become of us? How are we to support our poor children, now that we have nothing more for ourselves?"

"I'll tell you what, husband," answered the woman who was stepmother to Hansel and Gretel. "Early tomorrow morning we will take the children out into the thickest part of the woods. There we shall light a fire for them and give them each a piece of bread; then we'll go on to our work and leave them alone. They won't be able to find their way home, and we shall thus be rid of them."

"No, wife," said her husband, "that I won't do; how could I find it in my heart to leave my children alone in the woods? The wild beasts would soon come and tear them to pieces."

"Oh! You fool," she said, "then we must all four die of hunger, and you may just as well go and plane the boards for our coffins." And she left him no peace till he consented.

"But I can't help feeling sorry for the poor children," added the husband.

The children, too, had not been able to sleep for hunger, and had heard what their stepmother had said to their father. Gretel wept bitterly and spoke to Hansel. "Now we shall surely die."

"No, no, Gretel," said Hansel, "don't fret. I'll find a way to escape."

And when his father and step-mother had fallen asleep, he got up, slipped on his little coat, opened the back door and stole out. The moon was shining clearly, and the white pebbles which lay in front of the house glittered like bits of silver. Hansel bent down and filled his pocket with as many of them as he could. Then he went back and said to Gretel:

"Be comforted, my dear little sister, and go to sleep. God will not desert us." And he lay down in bed again.

At daybreak, even before the sun was up, the woman came and woke the two children:

"Get up, you lazy-bones, we're all going to the forest to fetch wood."

She gave them each a bit of bread and spoke:

"Here's something for your lunch, but don't eat it up too soon, for it's all you'll get."

Gretel put the bread under her apron, as Hansel had the stones in his pocket. Then they all set out together on the way to the forest.

After they had walked for a while, Hansel stood still and looked back at the house every so often. His father saw him and asked:

"Hansel, what are you gazing at there, and why do you always remain behind? Come along and don't lose your footing."

"Oh! father," said Hansel, "I am looking back at my white kitten, which is sitting on the roof, waving me a farewell."

The woman exclaimed:

"What a donkey you are! That isn't your kitten, that's the morning sun shining on the chimney."

But in fact Hansel had not looked back at his kitten. Rather he had always dropped one of the white pebbles out of his pocket onto the path.

When they had reached the middle of the forest, the father said:

"Now, children, go and fetch a lot of wood, and I'll light a fire so you won't be cold."

Hansel and Gretel heaped up brushwood till they had made a pile nearly the size of a small hill. The brushwood was set afire, and when the flames leaped high the woman said:

"Now lie down next to the fire, children, and rest yourselves. We are going into the forest to cut down wood. When we've finished we'll come back and get you."

Hansel and Gretel sat down beside the fire, and at midday ate their little bits of bread. They heard the strokes of the axe, so they thought their father was quite near. But it was no axe they heard, just a branch he had tied on to a dead tree that was blown about by the wind. After they had waited for a long time, their eyes closed with fatigue and they fell fast asleep.

When they awoke, it was pitch-dark. Gretel began to cry, and said:

"How are we ever going to get out of the woods?"

But Hansel comforted her.

"Wait a bit," he said, "till the moon is up, and then we'll find our way sure enough."

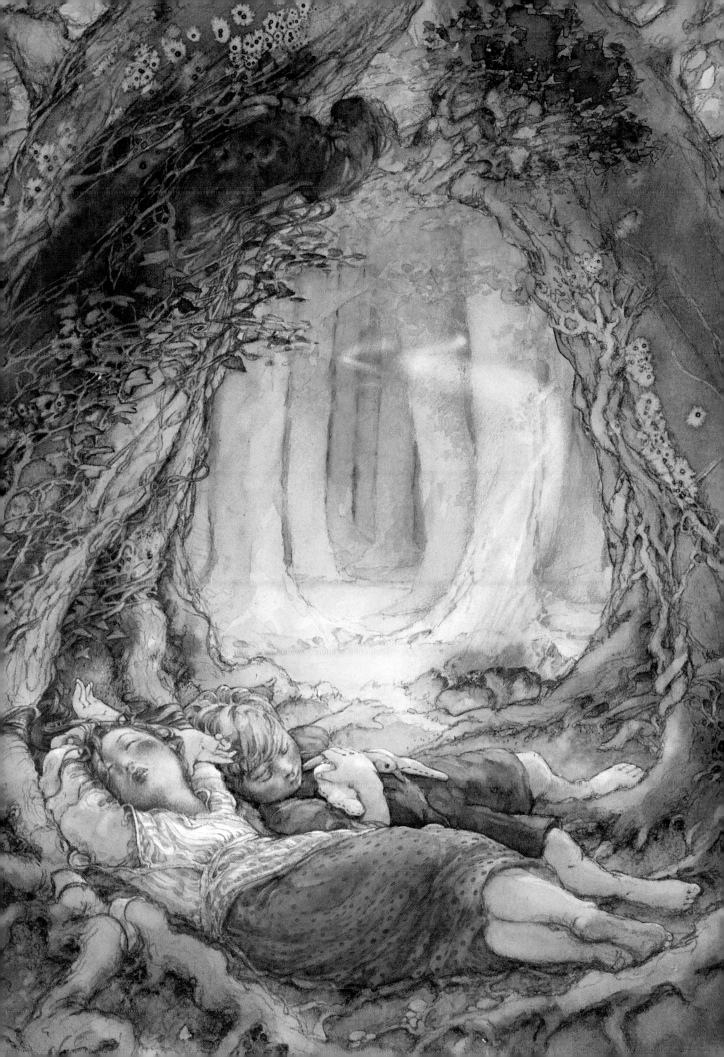

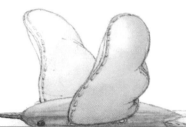

When the full moon had risen, he took his sister by the hand and followed the pebbles, which shone like new pennies and showed them the path. They walked all through the night, and at daybreak reached their father's house. They knocked at the door, and when the woman opened it she exclaimed:

"You naughty children, what a long time you've slept in the woods! We thought you were never going to come back."

But the father rejoiced, for he had felt guilty for leaving his children behind by themselves.

Not long afterwards there was again great famine in the land, and the children heard their stepmother address their father in bed one night:

"Everything is eaten up once more; we have only a half a loaf of bread in the house, and when that's gone we will starve. The children must be gotten rid of. We'll lead them deeper into the woods this time, so that they won't be able to find their way out again. There is no other way to save ourselves."

The man's heart sank at these words, and he thought:

"Surely it would be better to share the last bite of food with one's children!"

But his wife would not listen to his arguments, and did nothing but scold him. If a man yields once, he's done for. And because he had given in to his wife the first time, he was forced to do so the second.

The children were awake and had heard the conversation. When his father and stepmother were asleep, Hansel got up, and wanted to go out and pick up pebbles again, as he had done the first time; but the woman had barred the door, and Hansel couldn't get out. But he consoled his little sister, and said:

"Don't cry, Gretel, and sleep peacefully, for God is sure to help us."

At early dawn the woman came and made the children get up. They received their bit of bread, but it was even smaller than the time before. On the way to the woods, Hansel crumbled it in his pocket, and every few minutes he stood still and dropped a crumb on the ground.

"Hansel, what are you stopping and looking back for?" asked his father.

"I'm looking back at my little pigeon, which is sitting on the roof waving me farewell," answered Hansel.

"Fool!" said the wife, "that isn't your pigeon, it's the morning sun glittering on the chimney."

But Hansel gradually threw all his crumbs onto the path. The woman led the children still deeper into the forest, farther than they had ever been in their lives. Then a big fire was lit again, and the stepmother said:

"Just sit down there, children, and if you're tired you can sleep a bit; we're going into the forest to cut wood, and in the evening when we're finished, we'll come back to get you."

At midday Gretel divided her bread with Hansel, for he had dropped all of his along the path. Then they fell asleep, and evening passed away, but nobody came back for the poor children.

They didn't wake up till it was pitch-dark, and Hansel comforted his sister, saying:

"Just wait, Gretel, till the moon rises, then we shall see the breadcrumbs I scattered along the path; they will show us the way back to the house."

When the moon appeared they got up, but they found no crumbs, for the thousands of birds that fly about the woods and fields had picked them all up.

"Never mind," said Hansel to Gretel. "You'll see we will still find a way out."

They wandered about the whole night, and the next day, from morning till evening, but they could not find a path out of the woods. They were very hungry, too, for they had nothing to eat but a few berries they found growing on the bushes here and there. At last they were so tired that their legs refused to carry them any longer, so they lay down under a tree and fell asleep.

On the third morning after they had left their father's house, they set about their wandering again, but only got deeper and deeper into the woods. Now they felt that if help did not come soon, they would perish. At midday they saw a beautiful little snow-white bird sitting on a branch. It sang so sweetly that they stopped and listened to it. When its song was finished it flapped its wings and flew on in front of them. They followed it and soon came to a little house, where the bird perched on the roof.

And when they came quite near they saw that the cottage was made of bread and roofed with cakes, while the window was made of transparent sugar.

"Now," said Hansel, "we'll have a feast. I'll eat a bit of the roof, and you, Gretel, can eat some of the window which you will find a sweet morsel."

Hansel reached up and broke off a little bit of the roof to see what it was like, and Gretel went to the window, and began to nibble at it. Immediately a shrill voice called out from the room inside:

*"Nibble, nibble, little mouse,*
*Who is nibbling at my house?"*

The children answered:

*"Tis Heaven's own child,*
*The tempest wild,"*

and went on eating without worry. Hansel, who found the roof delicious, tore down a big part of it, while Gretel pushed out an entire round windowpane and sat down to enjoy it.

Suddenly the door opened, and an ancient woman leaning on a staff hobbled out. Hansel and Gretel were so terrified that they let what they had in their hands fall. But the old woman shook her head and said:

"Oh, ho! you dear children. Who led you here? Just come in and stay with me; no ill shall befall you."

She took them both by the hand and led them into the house, and laid a most sumptuous dinner before them—milk and sugared pancakes, with apples and nuts. After they had finished, two beautiful little white beds were prepared for them. When Hansel and Gretel lay down in them they felt as if they had gone to heaven.

The woman had appeared to be most friendly, but she was really an old witch who had waylaid the children, and had only built the little bread house in order to lure them in. When anyone fell under her spell she killed, cooked, and ate them, holding a regular feast-day for the occasion. Now witches have red eyes and cannot see far, but, like beasts, they have a keen sense of smell, and know when human beings pass by. When Hansel and Gretel fell into her hands, she laughed maliciously and said:

"I've got them now; they shan't escape me."

Early in the morning, before the children were awake, the witch arose. And when she saw them both sleeping so peacefully, with their round rosy cheeks, she muttered to herself:

"That'll be a dainty bite."

Then she seized Hansel with her bony hands and carried him into a little stable, and barred the door on him. He screamed as loudly as he could, but it did him no good. Then she went to Gretel, shook her till she awoke, and cried:

"Get up, you lazy-bones, fetch water and cook something for your brother. When he's fat I'll eat him up."

Gretel began to cry bitterly, but it was of no use; she had to do what the wicked witch told her.

So the best food was cooked for poor Hansel, but Gretel got nothing but crab-shells. Every morning the old woman hobbled out to the stable and cried:

"Hansel, stick out your finger, that I may feel if you are getting fat."

But Hansel always stretched out a bone, and the old woman, whose eyes were bad, couldn't see it, and thinking it was Hansel's finger, wondered why he fattened so slowly. When four weeks passed and Hansel still remained thin, she lost patience and decided to wait no longer.

"Gretel," she called to the girl, "be quick and get some water. Hansel may be fat or thin, but I'm going to kill him tomorrow and cook him."

Oh! How the poor little sister sobbed as she carried the water, and how the tears rolled down her cheeks!

"Kind heaven help us now!" she cried. "If only the wild beasts in the woods had eaten us, then at least we should have died together."

"Just hold your peace," said the old hag. "It won't help you."

Early in the morning, Gretel had to go out and hang up the kettle full of water and light the fire.

"First we'll bake," said the witch. "I've already heated the oven and kneaded the dough."

She pushed Gretel out to the oven, from which fiery flames already leapt.

"Creep in," said the witch, "and see if it's properly heated, so that we can shove in the bread."

For when she had gotten Gretel in, the old woman meant to close the oven and let the girl bake, so that she might eat her up too. But Gretel perceived her intention, and spoke:

"I don't know how I'm to do it; how do I get in?"

"You silly goose!" said the hag, "the opening is big enough. See, I could get in myself." And she crawled toward it, and poked her head into the oven.

Then Gretel gave her a shove that sent her right in, shut the iron door, and drew the bolt. Gracious! How she yelled! It was quite horrible. But Gretel fled, and the wretched old woman was left to perish miserably.

Then Gretel ran straight to Hansel, opened the little stabledoor, and cried:

"Hansel, we are free; the old witch is dead."

Then Hansel sprang like a bird out of a cage when the door is opened. How they rejoiced, and hugged each other, and jumped for joy, and kissed one another! And as they no longer had any cause for fear, they went to the old hag's house, and there they found, in every corner of the room, boxes of pearls and precious stones.

"These are even better than pebbles," Hansel said, and filled his pockets full of them; and Gretel said:

"I too will bring some of them home." And she filled her apron full.

"Now," said Hansel, "let's go and get well away from the witch's woods."

After they had wandered about for several hours, they came to a big lake.

"We can't get across it," said Hansel. "I see no bridge of any kind."

"Yes, and there's no ferry-boat either," answered Gretel. "But look, there swims a white duck; perhaps she'll help us over." So she called out:

> *"Here are two children,*
> *Mournful very,*
> *Seeing neither*
> *Bridge nor ferry;*
> *Take us upon*
> *Your white back,*
> *And row us over,*
> *Quack, quack!"*

The duck swam toward them, and Hansel got on her back and asked his little sister to sit beside him.

"No," answered Gretel, "we would be too heavy a load for the duck; she will have to carry us across separately."

The good bird did this, and when they were both safely on the other side, and had gone on for a while, the woods became more and more familiar to them, and after a while they saw their father's house in the distance.

Then they began to run, and bounding into the room, they hugged their father. The man had not passed a happy hour since he left them in the woods, but the woman had died. Gretel shook out her apron, and the pearls and precious stones rolled about the room, and Hansel also emptied his pockets one handful after another. Thus all their troubles were ended, and they all lived happily ever after.

My story is done. See! There runs a little mouse. Anyone who catches it may make himself a large fur cap out of it.